The Puzzle
of the Platypus

Scientists Probe 11 Animal Mysteries

The Puzzle of the Platypus

and Other Explorations of Science in Action

Jack Myers, Ph.D.
Senior Science Editor
HIGHLIGHTS FOR CHILDREN

Illustrated by John Rice

Boyds Mills Press
Honesdale, Pennsylvania

Photo credits: page 26—Chris Aikenhead; page 35—copyright © Behavioural Ecology Research Group, University of Oxford; page 43—Professor Heinz-Ulrich Reyer.

Illustration and graphic artwork credits: pages 16–17—based on a figure from W. L. Au (1993); page 46—based on a figure from H. A. Isack and H.-U. Reyer (1989).

Boyds Mills Press, Inc.
815 Church Street
Honesdale, Pennsylvania 18431
Printed in China

Library of Congress Cataloging-in-Publication Data

Myers, Jack.
  The puzzle of the platypus : and other explorations of science in action /
Jack Myers ; illustrated by John Rice.
    p. cm.
  ISBN 978-1-59078-556-0 (hardcover : alk. paper)
1. Animals—Miscellanea—Juvenile literature. 2. Zoology—Research—
Juvenile literature. I. Rice, John, ill. II. Title.

  QL49.M9439 2008
  590—dc22
                                   2007023741

First edition
The text of this book is set in 13-point Berkeley.
The illustrations are done in watercolor.

10 9 8 7 6 5 4 3 2

CONTENTS

Introduction

From the late 1950s until his death in 2006, Jack Myers, Ph.D., was the chief science editor at *Highlights for Children* magazine. With affection and respect, the staff at the magazine called him "Uncle Jack." Throughout those years, he gave his young readers the best true science stories he could find. Eleven of his articles are collected in this book, and many more are featured in four earlier books.

As a scientist, Uncle Jack knew the pleasures and frustrations of working to solve nature's mysteries, and he wanted others to imagine what those experiences must be like. So he told stories. He did not talk about his own accomplishments, although he had many. But he had a gift for telling the stories of others.

As a rule, Uncle Jack spent more time listening and thinking than he did talking, and he often seemed to be lost in thought. But when he told a story, he looked you in the eye and smiled. Sometimes he was so delighted by a clever experiment or a surprising result that he began to laugh to himself even before he had told you about it. And at the end of a story, he would often shake his head, appreciating the scientist's contribution the way someone else might linger over a perfect touchdown or painting or chess move.

One thing he loved more than telling science stories was learning about new ones. And science is full of new ones. They are happening all the time. As he discovered new stories, he told them to his friends and, especially, his readers.

In early years, Uncle Jack's stories were published under the heading of Science Reporting. That was a good title because each was based on an original and current report, such as those cited on page 62. Later, his articles in the magazine (and these books) took on the name Science in Action. That heading reminds the reader that science is not a collection of facts but, in his words, "an ongoing, self-correcting process."

When we began to collect the best of Uncle Jack's stories in these books, he made a thoughtful review of his many articles. He updated several of them, as needed. Some he left out. They were not up to the ever-rising standard he had set for himself. He also appreciated the new illustrations by John Rice. He enjoyed the "just-for-fun" illustrations at the beginning of each chapter, which suggest the topic at hand. And he thought they were well balanced by the true-to-life illustrations that follow.

Uncle Jack wanted others to love these stories as he did. Luckily for us, he wrote a lot of them.

Welcome to Science in Action.

Andy Boyles
Science Editor
Highlights for Children

Finding Polar-Bear Dens

A special camera spots them so we can protect them.

Mother polar bears give birth to their cubs in dens they have made by scooping out hollow spaces in snowbanks.

As people search for oil in Alaska, scientists have a problem: finding the dens so polar bears can be protected from road building and oil drilling. Solving that problem is a story about how discoveries in one part of science help progress in another part.

Mothers and Cubs

A denning polar bear puts out as much heat as a 200-watt light bulb. That's enough to protect against the extreme cold outside the den but not enough to make it toasty warm inside, not even to melt the snow blanket over the den.

Inside, the cubs begin their lives in temperatures just above freezing. Even so, that little heat from the mother can show as a slightly warmer spot in the snow above the den.

There is a neat way to tell the temperature of any object from the amount and "color" of the radiation it gives off. The Sun is an extreme example. Because it is so hot at thousands of degrees, we can see and feel its radiation as sunlight. Every object gives off radiation, depending on its temperature. For most objects, this radiation is such a dull "red" that our eyes can't see it. We call it *infrared* radiation. Scientists have gotten better and better at making detectors that can "see" infrared radiation. Some detectors can even make an infrared video.

"Bear Light"

A team of scientists led by Dr. Steven Amstrup tested the idea of using a warmer spot in a snowbank to tell about a polar-bear den underneath.

Their infrared video camera was mounted on the underside of a helicopter and pointed at the ground below. The scientists rode in the cabin of the helicopter, watching the video screen. The screen was adjusted to show the snowbank below as a gray smear.

Any place that was warmer, like the snow above a polar-bear den, appeared as a bright spot against the gray background.

Bright Spots

From their continued study of polar bears, the team knew about fifteen dens with bears that had been fitted with radio collars. While checking these fifteen dens from the air, the research team found eleven other "warm spots" that also showed up on their infrared video screens.

When the scientists checked those locations, all but three were found to be actual dens. The three "false positives" were caused by unexpected heat sources. For example, one was a big steel barrel and another was a boulder that had held a little heat from the previous summer. The twenty-three polar-bear dens were found over and over again.

The scientists concluded that infrared video gives a practical way to find and avoid the dens and help polar bears live with people.

Dolphins in Their Noisy World

To study their sonar, teach them a game.

In the seawater world of the dolphin, sound is the very best way to communicate or to learn about the surroundings—obstacles or prey or predators.

Scientists have studied two kinds of sounds that are a big part of dolphin life. One kind is a whistle, usually a few seconds long and in many different patterns. Among its many whistles, each dolphin has a special pattern—like a signature—that it uses to tell others where it is.

A very different dolphin sound is the click. That's a sharp burst less than one-thousandth of a second long. It is mostly ultrasonic (with a pitch too high for human ears) and used for sonar. By making that loud click and listening to the echoes, a dolphin can find out a lot about what's out there. That works especially well in water, where sound travels about five times faster than it does through air.

An echo may contain a lot of information. The direction of the echo tells the direction of an object that reflected the sound. The time delay tells about the distance the click traveled plus the distance for the echo to travel back. And the details of the echo may tell about what kind of object reflected it.

Dolphins are so good at using their sonar that lots of studies have been designed to find out how they do it.

A Sonar Game

As in most studies of animal abilities, scientists first teach the animal a game that it can play over and over. When scientists study dolphins, the game usually is designed to tell about how they use sonar. The illustration below shows a dolphin in a floating playpen specially designed for the game.

The best way to understand the game is to imagine that you are playing it yourself. You be the dolphin, and I'll be the trainer helping with the game.

You are blindfolded by rubber eyecups so that you can tell what's around you only through your ears. You have been trained to start in a special position with your head in a hoop, as shown in the illustration. A game trial starts when I pull a string and lower a sound-blocking screen out of the way. That's your cue to start making clicks and listening to their echoes.

Detecting the Target

Today's target is a 4-inch steel ball, but sometimes it may be much smaller. It may be hung at some measured distance in front of you. (In the illustration it is about 10 feet away.) My job is to control the target. It is suspended by fishing line so I can pull it up out of the way. The target is either there or not there. Your job is to use your sonar to tell which.

If you hear an echo from the target, you swim up and push the right paddle to say "It's there." If you can't hear any echo telling about the target, you swim up and push the left paddle to say "No, it's not there."

If your choice was correct, I press a buzzer that tells you to come up for a snack. (For a dolphin, that's a tasty fish.) If you have made the wrong choice, there is no buzzer and no reward.

You just swim back to the hoop and get ready for the next trial.

At first the game seems too easy. You can always hear echoes when the steel ball is there, and you never make a mistake when the target is not there.

The game gets harder as I move the target farther away and the echoes become weaker. Then you will begin making mistakes.

I move the steel ball way out to 230 feet—about three-fourths the length of a football field. At that distance, you can detect it only nine times in every ten trials. Now, every extra small distance makes the echoes harder to hear. At 240 feet, you are correct in your echo detection only about five times in every ten trials.

Mysteries of Sonar

Our game was taken from a book by Dr. Whitlow Au. He played the game for real with a dolphin named Sven in Kaneohe Bay, Hawaii. The illustration I used was taken from one of his experiments. From the results of the game, you can see that a dolphin can easily find a table-tennis ball in a big, Olympic-size swimming pool.

Dr. Au has gone on to do a whole book full of experiments on dolphin sonar. He trained dolphins to listen to echoes from a standard target and then tell when some other target was used instead. He has used targets of different shapes and different materials.

He is still searching for the dolphins' secret: how does a dolphin use echoes to learn if an object is round or flat, rough or smooth, and hard or soft?

Dr. Au has said: "The dolphin's ability to discriminate and recognize features of targets with its sonar is a characteristic that man-made sonar systems do not possess." By studying dolphins, he hopes to make man-made sonar as good as theirs.

The Puzzle of the Platypus

Bird? Reptile? Mammal?
No one knew what to call it.

The platypus is a furry, four-footed animal that lives in rivers near the eastern coast of Australia. It was well known to the early native Australians, the Aborigines. But it was a new and curious animal to the first Europeans who came to explore and later settle.

For scientists back in England, the process of discovering and understanding the platypus was so difficult that it went on for more than eighty years. Part of the problem was that each trip between Europe and Australia took more than a month at sea. More of the problem was in the animal's strange characteristics, which had never been seen together in one animal.

The first scientific description of the platypus was made from a preserved skin sent back to England. The report said: "A perfect resemblance of the beak of a duck grafted on the head of a quadruped." (A quadruped is a four-footed animal.) There was some worry that the animal was a fake—that the specimens had been put together from parts of different kinds of animals.

As other reports and other parts of the animal came to English scientists, the platypus became real but ever stranger. The back feet had pointy claws with a web of skin between them. The front feet had a web that extended even beyond the claws.

Furry "Amphibian"

People who had seen the platypus said that it made a living by diving to scoop up worms and crayfish between the long upper and lower lips of its bill. Onshore, it used its claws to dig burrows in the riverbank. It was amphibious, living both in water and on land.

Study of the platypus's insides showed that it has a cloaca, a structure found in birds and reptiles. This is an opening—a single opening for all body wastes, both feces and urine. In birds and reptiles, the cloaca also serves as a passageway for laying eggs.

Further study found glands that were much like the milk-producing mammary glands of mammals. Then, observations on living animals found actual production of milk. On the surface, the mammary glands were found to be small and not easily seen. And the nipples were covered with fur. But even very simple mammary glands became a key discovery because they are known only in the group of animals called mammals.

It Lays What?

There was another important question. How did it give birth? It took a long time to be sure of an answer. The Aborigines were certain that the platypus laid eggs. Scientists in England just couldn't believe that. Making milk for its babies and also laying eggs did not go together in any animal they knew about.

Lots of wild eggs were collected, and some were even shipped to England. But none ever gave rise to a baby platypus. One scientist in Australia did not believe the egg story and spent forty years looking for a live baby inside a mother platypus.

Throughout most of the 1800s, the platypus was in the science books but with a big question: What kind of animal was it? In 1884, Dr. William Caldwell, a young scientist at Cambridge University, set out for Australia. His job was to answer the platypus question by finding breeding animals.

After he arrived in Australia, Dr. Caldwell camped out along a river where the platypus was easy to find, then he enlisted some Aborigines to help. In August, during the breeding season, they helped him find female platypuses.

Hatching an Answer

Finally he found a female with an answer to his search. Her first egg had just been laid. The second egg was still there in the tube leading to the cloaca.

He opened the egg and found inside a developing embryo. It had reached a stage of development that he judged to be "equal to a thirty-six-hour chick" in a typical incubated chicken egg. So the platypus laid eggs, all right. But even before the eggs were laid, the embryos had already begun to develop.

Now all the pieces of the platypus puzzle were in. Scientists had a name for it, but how should they classify it? How could they fit this animal into the scheme that they had built for the whole animal kingdom?

They knew the platypus had four legs and no feathers, so it surely was not a bird. It was like the mammals in having mammary glands for milk, fur on the outside, and (as discovered later) a built-in temperature control so that it could be warm-blooded. It also had a cloaca and laid eggs like the reptiles. So where did it fit best?

Scientists decided in favor of mammary glands and fur. They placed the platypus in a special group of mammals, the monotremes ("one-opening" animals). This just says that of all the classes of animals, the platypus is most like the mammals. Then it says that they are different from other mammals in having only one opening in the body cavity.

Of course, the platypus never knew of all the scientific hubbub about what it was. And to this day it still lives happily in the rivers of eastern Australia.

Lee Boyd and the Wild Horses

Today she's helping to bring back
an endangered species.

Dr. Lee Boyd fell in love with horses when she was a little girl. Next to her home in Maryland was an open field that became a horse pasture. Every day she saw horses grazing, sometimes playing, right next door. At recess in her first years at school, she and her friends would pretend they were horses running free.

"I wanted a horse of my own," she says. "But my parents naturally were concerned whether I could take care of one. I got my father to build a wooden hobbyhorse, then I set a pail of water in front of it just to show I knew how. Finally, when I was in the third grade, my persistence was rewarded. We got a pony."

Interest in animals led her into biology. After college, she wanted to see the open spaces of the West. So she went to graduate school in Wyoming.

Mustangs

She wanted to study mountain lions until she saw mustang horses running wild on the plains.

She says that horses' behavior when they are in the wild is more interesting than when they are in pastures and stables. In the wild, horses must take care of themselves. They have to find watering places and grass for grazing. And they must learn how to avoid predators like wolves and mountain lions.

Though many mustangs are still running wild, they usually are not considered wild animals. They are descendants of horses that Spanish conquerors rode into America in the early 1500s.

Ms. Boyd's experience with mustangs led her into more graduate work at Cornell University. There, she studied under a famous veterinarian, Dr. Katherine Houpt.

Truly Wild Horses

After she earned her doctoral degree, Dr. Boyd found a position at Washburn University in Topeka, Kansas. The Topeka Zoo had the special attraction of ten truly wild horses.

These horses have never been tamed. They are not even the same species as domestic horses. They are smaller and usually lighter in color, with thick, short necks and manes that stick up. They were discovered in Mongolia in 1880 by the Polish explorer Nikolai Przewalski (sheh-VAHL-ski). Naturally, they have come to be called Przewalski's horses.

Even before Dr. Boyd first learned about them, Przewalski's

horses had a big problem. Only a few of them were left in the world. The native peoples of Mongolia had treated them as they did other wild animals. The people let their livestock crowd out the wild horses in competition for food and water. Then came severe winters with ice instead of snow. The last recorded sighting of a wild Przewalski's horse occurred in 1968.

But many years earlier, a few of the wild horses had been captured and taken to zoos and animal parks. These separate, small bands became the only Przewalski's horses left in the world.

Dr. Lee Boyd

Horse Lovers

Fortunately, there were two people in Holland who also loved wild horses. Jan and Inge Bouman created a foundation for the preservation of Przewalski's horses. They began to reestablish them in a park in Mongolia. Dr. Boyd's experience led her to become a key figure. She spent more than a thousand hours observing the horses and helping with management.

Dr. Boyd solved several problems to help Przewalski's horses live much as they would in the wild. For example, she helped give the horses more space to roam.

These efforts have paid off. Dr. Boyd says that there are over 170 Przewalski's horses living wild again in Hustai National Park of Mongolia. With aid from the foundation and from Washburn University, Dr. Boyd has visited the park six times.

"It's fantastic," she says. "I can follow wild horses on foot and see what they do day to day. I know their watering places, resting places, and favorite grazing places. I know many of the family groups, each of up to five mares and their young colts, led by a stallion."

When Dr. Boyd first visited Hustai, the Mongolian managers sought her advice about wolves. Wolves do not bother healthy adult horses but can easily kill newborn foals. What should be done? Dr. Boyd told them about the history of wolves in the United States. "Please don't make the same mistake we did," she said. "We used to kill off wolves to protect grazing animals. Now we are trying to reintroduce wolves to keep the balance of nature."

So far it's working. Horse families have learned to protect their young from predators by forming a circle around the foals.

Dr. Boyd looks forward to those visits with Mongolian wild horses. I think of her as the woman who loves horses.

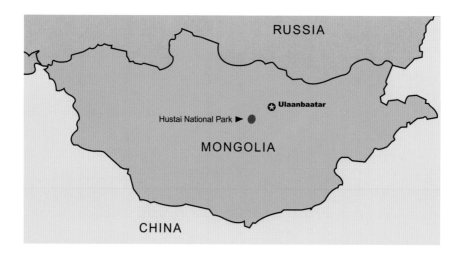

Elephant Grandmothers

In elephant families, everyone listens to Grandma.

When Dr. Karen McComb came to Amboseli National Park in East Africa, her first task was to learn the names of the one hundred or so elephants most often seen.

Scientists working in the park have learned to study elephants up close by watching them from Land Rovers. They have a catalog of the park's almost one thousand elephants, identified mainly by shapes and markings on their ears and tusks. When the scientists started the catalog, they gave each elephant a number until they discovered that remembering individuals by name is easier than by number. There are estimates of age for all of the elephants and even actual records (like birth certificates) for all born since 1972.

Amboseli was a good place for Dr. McComb to study animal communications, and elephants were a great subject because their lifestyle depends so much on communication.

An Eating Lifestyle

Elephants make their living eating grasses and plant leaves. It takes a lot—about three hundred pounds a day for a grown-up. That means elephants need to keep moving around just to find enough food. And eating takes a lot of time—more than half of each day is spent munching food and looking for more.

Big elephants are rough and tough enough that they don't have to worry about predators like lions. And there are not many diseases that threaten their lives. So elephants are generally long-lived animals. In big parks like Amboseli, where they are protected from human hunters, some live to be more than seventy years old. The real dangers to an elephant come when it is less than a year old. An elephant that young is small enough to walk under its mother's belly. It is also in danger from big predators or even other elephants.

Elephant Families

To make possible their continuous search for food and to protect their calves, most elephants live in small family groups. A typical family group is composed of about six adult females together with their calves, both male and female. When the males get to be about fifteen years old, they leave their families and go off to live in all-male groups. The family always has an old, old grandmother, the matriarch, who is the acknowledged leader.

The whole group of scientists began a regular routine of spending much of each day driving through the park in Land Rovers, watching the elephants and listening to how they communicate. In searching for food, an elephant often drifts away from the rest of its family. Then it keeps in touch by special "contact calls," just to learn what others in the family are doing.

The scientists saw that an elephant had a characteristic response when it heard a contact call from another member of its family. By holding out its ears, it would show that it was listening and then might give its own contact call in reply. Elephants have deep voices, mostly infrasonic, with only some of their sound vibrations in the range of human hearing. They can easily hear one another from more than a mile away.

Strangers or Friends?

There were times when two families came within each other's calling range. How would elephants respond to calls from members of other families?

To find out, the scientists used "playback" experiments. First they used microphones to record the contact calls of twenty different females. Then they watched a chosen family through binoculars while they played back a recorded call from an amplifier on their Land Rover.

Their notes and videotapes showed a wide range of responses. Some families showed a simple listening response. Other families seemed agitated, and nervously bunched together while their calves moved closer into the bunch. It was easy to see that a family could distinguish between other families by their calls.

Fortunately, the park records of many years showed how often a family had been seen and how often it had been seen with another family. That gave a scale of familiarity—from close friends to total strangers. The calls from a friendly family gave a simple listening response. Calls from strange families were recognized with a nervous bunching response.

Wise Elephants

Dr. McComb and her team had learned a great deal about how elephants communicate, but they kept on thinking about one puzzling observation. Some families were "smarter," or better at distinguishing calls of friends from those of strangers.

What made some families smarter than others? The scientists searched their records for an explanation. To their surprise, there was only one factor of importance: the "smartest" families always had the oldest matriarchs. Evidently a family, as it did in all other activities, waited for some signal from the matriarch before responding to a strange contact call. And older, more experienced matriarchs were better at telling whether other elephants were strangers or friends just by their calls.

That was an important discovery. It showed how an elephant family depends on the experience carried in the long memory of the matriarch.

Dr. McComb had started out to learn a little more about elephant communication. What she discovered was a much bigger idea about the importance of grandmothers in the lives of elephants.

A Toolmaking Crow

To get a treat, she had to be inventive.

Tools are so necessary for our way of life that we seldom think about how important they are. Try to imagine building a house out of wood without using any tools.

We once thought that only humans were smart enough to make and use tools. Scientists who were studying animals in nature wondered if that was true. They began looking for tool-making by other animals. A number of cases have been found. A recently reported one is fun to think about.

Playful Birds

Scientists at Oxford University—Dr. Alex A. S. Weir, Dr. Jackie Chappell, and Dr. Alex Kacelnik—began to study a pair of New Caledonian crows kept in a laboratory. In the wild this kind of crow often makes tools out of twigs and leaves. In the laboratory, the two crows played with common objects, which became their toys.

One day, the scientists set up a special problem, which you can see in the photo below. A little bucket inside a plastic pipe contained food (a piece of meat). At first, the crows were given a choice between straight wires and wires bent into hooks. The birds quickly realized that hooks worked better than straight wires for lifting out the bucket.

In one trial, the male took away the hooked wire. The female used her beak to bend a piece of straight wire into a hook.

Could She Do It Again?

That trick of making a hook looked so smart that the scientists tried to see if she could do it again. In repeated trials, they gave her only straight wire. If she wanted to get the meat, she would have to bend the wire into a hook. In seventeen trials, she succeeded nine times. The male crow sometimes stole one of the hooks his mate had made, but he never learned to make one himself.

Let's think about the accomplishment of that crow in making a hook as a special tool. Of course, if you had thought to do that, you likely would have been proud of yourself. But for a crow to do it—scientists considered that so remarkable that they took photos and wrote a scientific account.

It is clear enough that another animal can make a tool. But those tools are quite simple compared to the ones we make. You can see why the human is considered the "toolmaking" animal.

Parrots That Eat Dirt

Why do they do it?

In all the world there are just a few special places to see many colorful parrots in the wild. The most famous is at a bend of the Manu River in southern Peru, a small spot in the vast Amazon rain forest.

Early each morning a thousand or more parrots can be seen as they come to a bank of the river. These are the large chattery parrots also called macaws. Most of them are red and green, but there are other kinds with yellow and blue or scarlet feathers mixed in. Bird watchers come from all over the world to see the sight of those birds on display.

The idea of all those parrots coming together naturally leads to a question: what brings them? Just watching gives a surprising answer. They are eating dirt from the riverbank.

The Dirt They Eat

This is not just any old dirt. They carefully pick out a special layer that runs along the bank. By learning to recognize particular parrots, watchers can see that many come for their breakfast of dirt almost every day.

We live in sheltered homes and eat carefully prepared foods. For most of us, the idea of eating dirt seems distasteful or, you could say, just plain dirty. But for wild animals it is common enough that there is even a special word for it: geophagy.

Dr. James Gilardi, a scientist studying the wild parrots, set out to find out why they were eating that special dirt. Were the parrots seeking soil minerals that were low in their foods? No, there were no needed minerals in the favorite soil that were not also in their foods.

Some birds use geophagy just to get grit (pebbles or coarse sand) to help their gizzards grind up food. But that didn't fit the special soil layer the parrots were choosing. They liked a layer that was mostly smooth clay with tiny particles down to sizes of a millionth of an inch. So the parrots were not eating soil for its grit or minerals.

Dr. Gilardi kept at it until he found an explanation for the parrots' geophagy. The answer starts with an understanding of their other eating habits.

Bitter Foods

Parrots eat a lot of the fruit of forest trees. Fleshy fruits (think of peaches) are invitations to be eaten by animals. But the seeds inside are doubly protected. They are hard and tough. They also contain special chemicals called alkaloids that make them bitter or even poisonous if broken up.

Most animals chew up only the fleshy part of the fruit but pass

the whole seeds into their feces. For the plants, that's a great system. Their seeds are unharmed, and the animals do them a great service by scattering their seeds.

A seed contains a little embryo plant all ready to grow. It also has a storehouse with enough food to get it started. By not chewing up those protected seeds, most animals are losing some very good food. But not parrots. They have hard bills and strong jaws that can crunch even the hardest seeds.

Parrots seem to have a special food source all to themselves. They can break the tough seed coats and chew up the seeds of forest trees. But there is that second part of the seeds' defense. How do the parrots live with the poisonous alkaloids inside the seeds?

The Contents of Clay

Dr. Gilardi wondered if eating clay had something to do with that problem. He knew that naturally occurring clay has some special properties. It is made of small particles that carry a negative electric charge. Its particles can bind positively charged molecules, such as those of alkaloids. In a parrot's stomach, even a small amount of clay might bind the alkaloids and keep them from being poisonous.

To test his idea Dr. Gilardi did a simple experiment. Eight captive parrots were fed pills of a mildly poisonous alkaloid called quinidine. Eight other parrots were fed the same pills together with a small measured spoonful of clay. Then blood samples from all the parrots were analyzed to see how much of the quinidine was taken up by the parrots' bodies.

The answer was clear. The birds that were also given clay took up only about one-third as much quinidine. Eating clay is the parrots' way of living with the alkaloids of seeds.

Amazonian parrots have been getting special attention because they are decreasing in numbers. Many are being captured by native peoples to be sold as pets.

If it were not for the endangering effects of people, the parrots of the Amazon would have it made. They have a favorite and almost private food source in the seeds of forest trees. To prevent stomachache from the alkaloid poisons of the seeds, all they need is a breakfast of clay once a day from a riverbank.

People Who Eat Dirt

Geophagy is not exclusive to wild animals. People eat dirt, too.

There are many plants that would be good food except for their bitter or poisonous chemicals. Acorns, the seeds of oak trees, have their own special protection in chemicals called tannins. A few peoples of the world have learned to solve that problem and use acorns for food. The Pomo Indians of California have records of a recipe of a special bread made from acorns ground up and baked with some clay.

High up in the Andes Mountains of South America, one of the few sources of food is a wild potato that also has bitter alkaloids. People who live there have learned to eat bitter potatoes by cooking them with clay.

And even drugstores have stomachache medicine that contains clay as a main ingredient. It may be listed as *attapulgite*.

Honey Guides

These birds can lead people to honey.

The peoples of Africa have used honey as a part of their diet for thousands of years. That means searching for the hives of honeybees in such places as hollow trees and anthills out in the wild. There's a special story about how they do this.

There also lives in Africa a bird called the greater honey guide. It feeds on insects and has a special liking for the beeswax of the honeycomb that bees make for storing their honey. But getting pieces of honeycomb out of a bees' hive, or nest, is hard to do. The honey guide has found a way to get help doing that.

A Combined Effort

The birds and some of the peoples of Africa have become team players. The birds help people find bees' nests to get honey. People know how to use smoky fire to quiet the bees. And they use tools to open up the nests. Of course, the people take out most of the honey. But they leave lots of pieces of the comb and most of the bee larvae.

That's a neat story that has been told many times. But is it all really true? Do the birds really serve as guides? Two scientists, Dr. Hussein Isack and Dr. Heinz-Ulrich Reyer, studied the partnership of the birds and the people.

A Boran honey gatherer calls for a honey guide.

They conducted their study in northern Kenya. There, the pastoralist Boran people still make their living in the wild and still go in search of wild bees' nests as a source of honey. Dr. Isack is a native Boran and could talk to the men who gathered the honey.

The honey gatherers told about the birds' calls and flying patterns and what the birds did to guide them to a nest. Then to find out what really happened, the scientists watched and kept records on trips to seventy-four different nests.

Calling All Honey Gatherers

The Borans would make a special whistling sound, called Fuulido. It could be heard for over half a mile and was a signal to tell a bird they needed help. When a honey guide came, it gave its own rapid call, like *tirr-tirr-tirr-tirr*, to tell that the game was on.

Then it flew off above the treetops and was gone for a minute or more. The scientists concluded that this was a check-out flight to make sure of the direction of the nearest hive.

Soon the bird would be back, calling and perching where it could easily be seen. After that the bird would fly ahead, then perch and call. Everyone else would follow. Then the bird would fly ahead again to a new perch. The scientists kept track of the compass direction of each new flight, how far it was, and how high above the ground the honey guide perched.

Although the trips were not alike in time or in distance, they all had a common pattern. As the bird got closer to a hive, its behavior changed. Its flights became shorter, and it perched closer to the ground. Finally, its flights became very short, back and forth around the nest. By this time its call had changed to a softer tone and a longer spacing between notes.

A Guided Tour

There has been a common idea that the honey guides were really "finders" instead of "guides." The belief was that they probably flew around just searching, maybe looking for bees returning to a nest. That would work at least part of the time in leading people to a nest. But that was not how the birds behaved. They were not just looking for a nest. They led the way in an almost straight course, not hunting around.

You can see that in the sketch made of a typical trip. The birds had to know where they were going. They even gave hints about how far it was to the nest by the length of their flights and the height of their perches.

You can see why the scientists concluded that honey guides really are guides, bringing people to nests that the birds already know about.

We now have a scientific account based on careful records and measurements. The scientists noted that everything they had learned was just what the native honey gatherers had told them they would find. That was no surprise. Scientists have often found that native peoples living in the wild are great teachers in telling about the animals and plants around them.

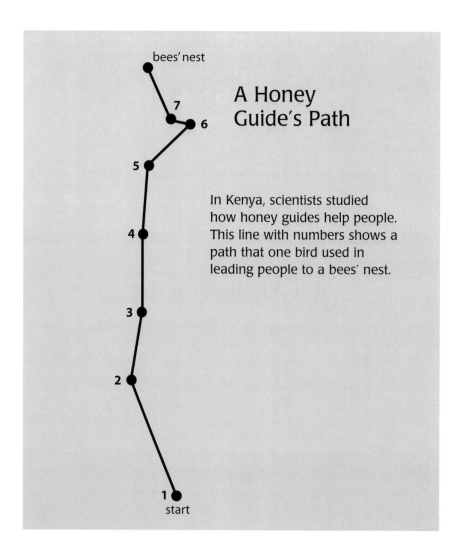

bees' nest

A Honey
Guide's Path

In Kenya, scientists studied
how honey guides help people.
This line with numbers shows a
path that one bird used in
leading people to a bees' nest.

start

When a Bowerbird Seeks a Mate

Why does he work so hard?

To scientists, bowerbirds may be the world's most famous birds—famous not for their looks but for their behavior.

Each male builds an elaborate bower as a place where he can show off to females in his search for a mate. The bower may be a platform or even a little building made by weaving together twigs and grass stems. Then he decorates the bower with any pretty things he can find.

In each of the several species of bowerbirds, the males have a distinctive way of building and tending their bowers. Tending is important because the males are always trying to steal decorations from one another.

Watching Wild Birds

To see bowerbirds in action, many scientists have taken long trips to the wild places where the birds live. That means the lands where northern Australia and southern Asia almost come together.

Dr. Gerald Borgia and a team of scientists have been going there to study in detail one species, the satin bowerbird. They have used automatic video cameras and have even done some experiments to try to understand the birds' special behaviors.

The male satin bowerbird makes a bower with two parallel walls about four inches apart and with a platform at its north end, all decorated with pretty things like colored feathers, flowers, and snail shells.

Doing Experiments

In one experiment the scientists divided twenty-two bowers into two groups. In one group they removed all decorations. Then they recorded the number of visits by females. The results came out fifteen to three in favor of the group with decorations.

The next year the scientists added different kinds of decorations to see which ones the females preferred. The winners were blue feathers and snail shells. Males fight with one another for these preferred decorations. So in picking males with the prettiest bowers, females are mating with the strongest males.

Why the Song and Dance?

The females also have a special set of behaviors, which occur in three stages. First, a female inspects and compares a whole series of bowers, usually when the males are away.

In a second stage, the female comes back to each of several selected bowers and watches from inside as the male does a vigorous song and dance on the platform in front. Then she leaves and spends about a week building a nest. Finally, she returns to the bower of the male she has chosen as her mate.

The scientists wondered about the first stages of courtship. Which was most important to the female in making her choice? Was it the prettiness of the bower or the song and dance?

By keeping track of females, scientists found that older birds chose mainly the performance. But the younger birds seemed afraid of a male's vigorous dance routine and made their choice based just on the decorations of the bower.

Scientists had been puzzled as to why the male bowerbird has so many different parts to his elaborate courtship. Now it is clear that the answer lies in the different ways that female bowerbirds make their choices.

Why Do Cliff Swallows Live Together?

Living close together has good points and bad points.

Most of the birds we see build their nests in lonely, hard-to-find places. Most birdsongs are really bird language that says: "Stay away. This place is mine." So there's a surprise in thinking about cliff swallows because they nest close together.

Cliff swallows get part of their name from a habit of attaching their mud nests to the faces of rock cliffs. They have found that many man-made sites are even better than rock cliffs—wooden barns, stucco houses, and (best of all) highway bridges. Even with all the room at those nesting sites, they choose to build their nests so close together that they form bird cities, or colonies. Some of these colonies have thousands of nests.

Cliff-Swallow Experts

Dr. Charles Brown and his wife, Mary, have found cliff swallows so interesting that they have been studying them for more than twenty-five years. They and their students have a great study site in southern Nebraska, with more than 150 colonies that vary in size from two nests to six thousand nests. The research has centered on a question that Dr. Brown puts very simply: "Why do cliff swallows live in colonies?"

Answering that question has taken a lot of work that is still going on. The scientists use ladders to get up close to the nests. Then they look inside, using flashlights and little mirrors like the ones dentists use to look at your teeth. They put leg bands on the adult birds for identification, and they use marker pens to keep track of nestlings. So they have learned a bookful of information about the private lives of cliff swallows through the stages of mating, nest building, egg laying, and bringing up nestlings.

A key to why these birds live in colonies has to do with how they find their food. Cliff swallows make their living by catching flying insects, especially tiny insects like mosquitoes that often fly close together in swarms. So an important part of hunting for food is to find an insect swarm. Some swarms can be as far as a mile from the nest.

Once eggs have hatched in late spring, bringing food for the usual three or four nestlings is almost more than a full-time job for the parents. By watching individual birds, scientists found that most parents were making a hunting trip and food delivery about once every four minutes most of the day.

A parent may have a hard time finding that much food. To do it, birds watch their neighbors. The scientists noticed that a bird that came home from a hunting trip without finding food seemed to know what to do. It watched neighbors to see who had been successful. Then it followed the lucky neighbor on its next flight. In larger colonies it is even easier because there is usually a steady stream of birds watching others and finding their way to the best hunting site. Thinking of the big advantage the swallows get by living together, Dr. Brown called the colony an information center because it allows birds to pool information to help everyone.

Blood-Sucking Bugs

The Browns also found some disadvantages of colony living. Cliff swallows have a problem with a blood-sucking parasite called a swallow bug. It has no wings but travels by clinging to the feet of adult swallows. It has long needle-like mouth parts and uses them to take blood from tender nestlings.

Scientists studied the effect of the swallow bugs by counting them—sometimes as many as two thousand in a nest. Then they weighed the nestlings. They found that nests with the most bugs had the smallest nestlings. Some of the babies were so puny that they would not survive their loss of blood to the parasites.

One other important result came out when the scientists checked their records. Close-packed colonies with the most nests also had the most bugs per nest. So the effects of parasites create a disadvantage to colony living but not enough to outweigh the advantages.

By showing these (and other) advantages and disadvantages of nesting close together, the Browns make it understandable why cliff swallows choose colonies of different sizes for their nests. Each time a bird picks a nest site, it must choose between a big colony (with lots of information but lots of swallow bugs) or a small colony (with fewer bugs but less information). Not all birds make the same choice.

It even looks as if a bird's choice of where to live is inherited from its parents. Each bird prefers to nest in a colony that's about the same size as its birth colony.

Most importantly, Dr. Brown has shown that most cliff swallows nest close together because of the big advantage of the colony as an information center that helps everyone.

How About Us?

Like cliff swallows, many people live close to one another. What do you think are the disadvantages of living in a city? What are the advantages?

How Rattlesnakes Make a Living

Here's a new way to think about them.

Almost no one loves a rattlesnake. It's not a cuddly animal and not one to make you stop and play. But even though you may want to stay away, you can admire the rattlesnake as an animal finely tuned in to nature.

There are a lot of different kinds of rattlesnakes that live in a wide variety of places, from forests to deserts. A feature they all have in common is that they are ambush predators. They lie quietly with head slightly raised, camouflaged by their coloration, waiting for a mouse or other small prey.

If a big animal comes by, a rattlesnake usually shakes its tail rattles. That makes the loud buzz that scares away large animals like deer or people. With big animals, the rattlesnake is always on the defensive.

As an ambush hunter the rattlesnake is equipped with a special form of "night vision." At the front of its head and just below the eyes are two little pits. At the back of the pits are membranes sensitive to heat radiation. These membranes have nerves leading to the brain. So even on the darkest night, a warm-blooded mouse shows up as a target.

The strike, which takes place in hundredths of a second, is not really a bite. It ends up as an injection of poisonous venom by fangs swung out from the back of the mouth.

After the strike, the very scared mouse is likely to run. The snake can't outrun a mouse. But it doesn't need to. Instead it quietly follows, flicking out its tongue to pick up the scent trail of the mouse.

Meanwhile, the injected poison is doing its job. At the end of the trail there will be a dead mouse. Eating is as quick as swallowing, although that may take awhile if the prey is bigger around than the snake. The snake can open its mouth wide enough to squeeze in an animal as big as a rabbit.

Sidewinders

To most rattlesnakes, meals don't come on schedule and don't come very often. The sidewinder rattlesnake of the California and Arizona deserts often goes for a month between meals. Then the sidewinder may eat a mouse or a ground squirrel that weighs half its own weight.

Scientists who were studying digestion in animals did some special research to find out how the snakes managed that kind of an eating schedule. Dr. Stephen M. Secor, Dr. Eric D. Stein, and Dr. Jared Diamond, all of the University of California at Los Angeles Medical School, were surprised by the results.

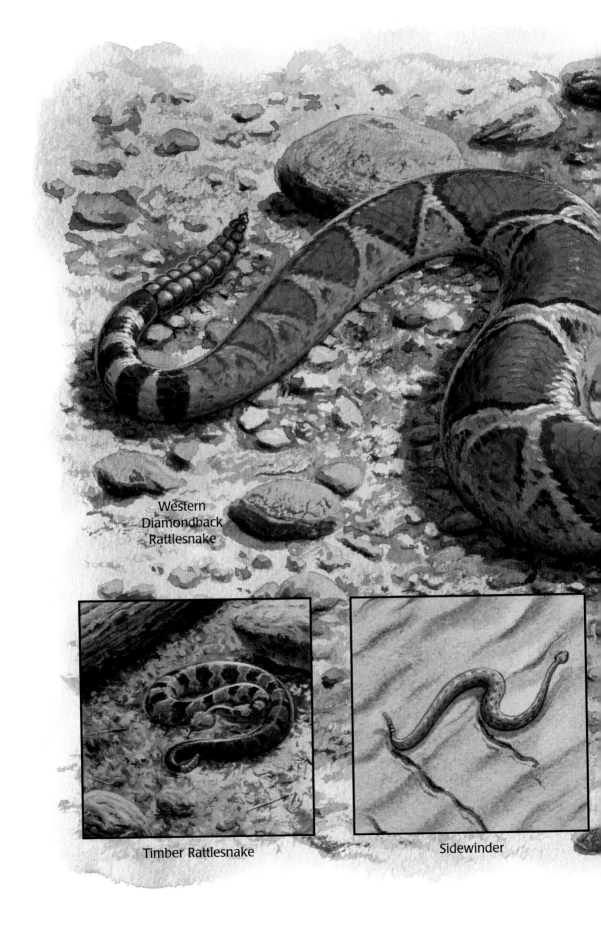

Western
Diamondback
Rattlesnake

Timber Rattlesnake

Sidewinder

Nostrils

Heat-sensing pits

Within two days after a mouse meal, the lining of the snake's intestine increased in thickness as much as three times. At the same time, its digestive activities and its total rate of energy expenditure increased more than five times.

It took two weeks for the snake to digest that big meal. Then the activities inside the snake's body slowed down to their very low resting levels.

Helpful Changes

What good do these changes offer the snake? When a rattlesnake eats a mouse, the digestive system has a big job to do. And so do other parts of the body, which have to distribute and store the food as it's digested.

After the mouse is digested, the thick intestinal lining and high energy rate are no longer needed. So the snake's body cuts back on both until the next meal.

The scientists studied other snakes that also go for long periods between meals. They found that these snakes have a similar drop in activity between meals and the expected increase in energy use right after a meal.

Diamondbacks

A scientist at the University of Arizona, Dr. Daniel D. Beck, has spent a lot of time in the Arizona mountains studying diamondbacks, the largest of the North American rattlesnakes. He caught fourteen adults and used surgery to put tiny radio transmitters inside them. That helped him keep track of them and record their activities for up to fifteen months.

The diamondbacks were not big travelers. In their summer and fall active seasons they spent only about twenty minutes each day roaming a total of about 150 feet. They did a lot of resting under cover of a rock or crevice. And they spent almost half their time quietly alert and waiting for their next meal to come by.

Measured rates of the use of energy by rattlesnakes are low compared to other snakes and lizards—and very low compared to small mammals.

One way to think about that for a meat-eating animal is to ask how much meat (or prey) the animal has to eat each year to survive. Measurements show that an adult diamondback rattlesnake needs an amount of prey a little less than its own weight. Just for comparison, a warm-blooded cat needs to eat about ten times its own weight every year.

We like to think about the wonderful advantage that people and cats and other warm-blooded animals have over cold-blooded animals. We can be active all year long because our bodies can control our body temperature.

But we pay a high price for that warm-blooded advantage in greater food requirements for our higher-energy lifestyle. To scientists, the rattlesnake is worthy of study because it is typical of animals with a slower and more economical lifestyle.

BIBLIOGRAPHY

Finding Polar-Bear Dens
Amstrup, S. C., G. York, T. L. McDonald, R. Nielson, and K. Simac. 2004. Detecting denning polar bears with forward-looking infrared (FLIR) imagery. *BioScience* 54:337–344.

Dolphins in Their Noisy World
Au, W. L. *The Sonar of Dolphins.* New York: Springer-Verlag, 1993.

The Puzzle of the Platypus
Grant, T. *The Platypus: A Unique Mammal.* 2nd ed. Sydney: University of New South Wales Press, 1995.

Hall, B. K. 1999. Thinking of biology: the paradoxical platypus. *BioScience* 49:211–218.

Lee Boyd and the Wild Horses
Boyd, L., and K. A. Houpt, eds. *The Przewalski's Horse: The History and Biology of an Endangered Species.* Albany: State University of New York Press, 1994.

Elephant Grandmothers
McComb, K., C. Moss, S. M. Durant, L. Baker, and S. Sayialel. 2001. Matriarchs as repositories of social knowledge in African elephants. *Science* 292:491–494.

McComb, K., C. Moss, S. Sayialel, and L. Baker. 2000. Unusually extensive networks of vocal recognition in African elephants. *Animal Behaviour* 59:1103–1109.

A Toolmaking Crow
Weir, A. A. S., J. Chappell, and A. Kacelnik. 2002. Shaping of hooks in New Caledonian crows. *Science* 297:981.

Parrots That Eat Dirt
Diamond, J. M. 1999. Co-evolution: dirty behavior. *Nature* 400:120–121.

Gilardi, J. D., S. S. Duffey, C. A. Munn, and L. A. Tell. 1999. Biochemical functions of geophagy in parrots: detoxification of dietary toxins and cytoprotective effects. *Journal of Chemical Ecology* 25:897–922.

Honey Guides
Isack, H. A., and H.-U. Reyer. 1989. Honeyguides and honey gatherers: interspecific communication in a symbiotic relationship. *Science* 243:1343–1346.

When a Bowerbird Seeks a Mate
Borgia, G. 1985. Bower quality, number of decorations and mating success of male satin bowerbirds (*Ptilonorhynchus violaceus*): an experimental analysis. *Animal Behaviour* 33:266–271.

Coleman, S. W., G. L. Patricelli, and G. Borgia. 2004. Letters: Variable female preferences drive complex male displays. *Nature* 428:742–745.

Why Do Cliff Swallows Live Together?
Brown, C. R., and M. B. Brown. *Coloniality in the Cliff Swallow: The Effect of Group Size on Social Behavior.* Chicago: University of Chicago Press, 1996.

How Rattlesnakes Make a Living
Beaupre, S. J., and D. J. Duvall. 1998. Integrative biology of rattlesnakes. *BioScience* 48:531-538.

Beck, D. D. 1995. Ecology and energetics of three sympatric rattlesnake species in the Sonoran Desert. *Journal of Herpetology* 29:211–223.

Secor, S. M., E. D. Stein, and J. Diamond. 1994. Rapid upregulation of snake intestine in response to feeding: a new model of intestinal adaptation. *American Journal of Physiology* 266:695–705.

INDEX